Tango Guitar Method

BY GUILLERMO MARIGLIANO

This book is dedicated to my wife, my daughter and my parents

Online Access Video: https://www.guillermomarigliano.com/content/

User: tangobook   Pass: Content*2023

Foreword

This book has been written for the guitarist who wants to learn how to play and perform on the guitar this Argentinian music style, which in its tradition and since its inception, has the guitar as the leading instrument of the genre, along with the bandoneon, the piano and the violin.

This method is useful both for the guitarist and musician who wants to perform as solo guitar, as well as for the one who wants to learn how to accompany singing with the instrument.

It is expected that the student will have a knowledge of the elements of written music: rhythmic notation, time signatures, basic scales, bar chords and tablature.

What the student will find in the content of this book is a guide to learn from the basic rhythms to the most complex, through the different rhythmic variants and characteristic harmonic forms that Tango has as a sty-le.

In addition to the progressions and rhythms, you will find the vocabulary of melodic musical ornaments, substitutions, introductions, link phrases, ending phrases, which will lead you to learn the style and develop your own vocabulary.

In order to integrate this knowledge and begin to master the style, it is necessary and very important (as for any style of music that you want to learn) to learn classic compositions of the genre, where you can turn these examples. I personally recommend listening to the recordings of Carlos Gardel, the Aníbal Troilo quartet, the Royal Quintet, the Osvaldo Pugliese orchestra and the Astor Piazzolla quintet.

It is my wish with this book, to contribute to art, music and teaching, and to help all those guitarists who want to immerse themselves in the interpretation of Tango as another form of expression within art and music.

Good luck with learning, practicing and performing.

Sincerely,

Guillermo Marigliano.

About the Autor

Guillermo Marigliano, a guitarist, composer, and producer, has been instructing in colleges and music organizations for more than 25 years

After receiving his Professional Guitar Degree, and his Jazz Arrange & Compostion Degree, he continues mastering his knowledge as a musician with his mentor Francisco Rivero.

His professional career started in Argentina, and after six albums released with original compositions movie soundtracks and three teaching books published, he's now continuing his career based in Los Angeles, California since 2021

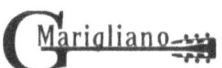

CHAPTER 1

COMPING RHYTHM

1) BASIC PATTERNS

TANGO MUSIC IS COMPOSED IN 4/4 TIME, WITH FOUR QUARTER NOTES EVERY BAR. THE FIRST PATTERN WE SHOULD MASTER IS "MARCATO," WHICH REQUIRES US TO PLAY THE FOUR QUARTER NOTES WITH THE SAME DYNAMIC ON EACH BEAT WHILE MAKING A SLIGHT RIGHT HAND MUTE.

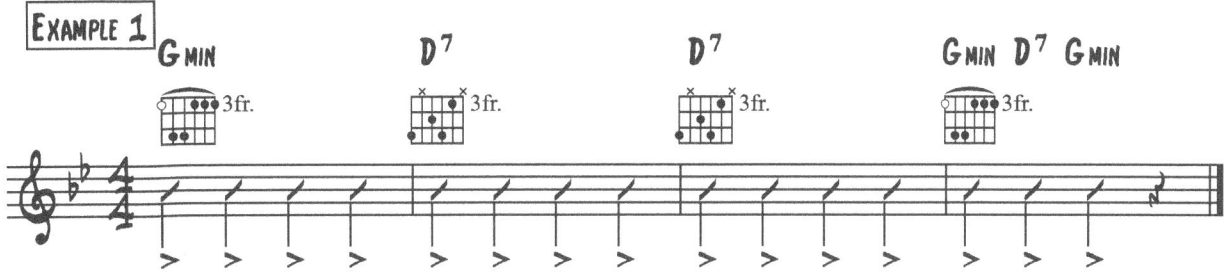

"MARCATO IN TWO TIMES," WE HIT THE FOUR QUARTER NOTE BEATS, BUT NOW WE'RE GOING TO EMPHASIZE BEATS 1 AND 3 WHILE MUTING BEATS 2 AND 4.

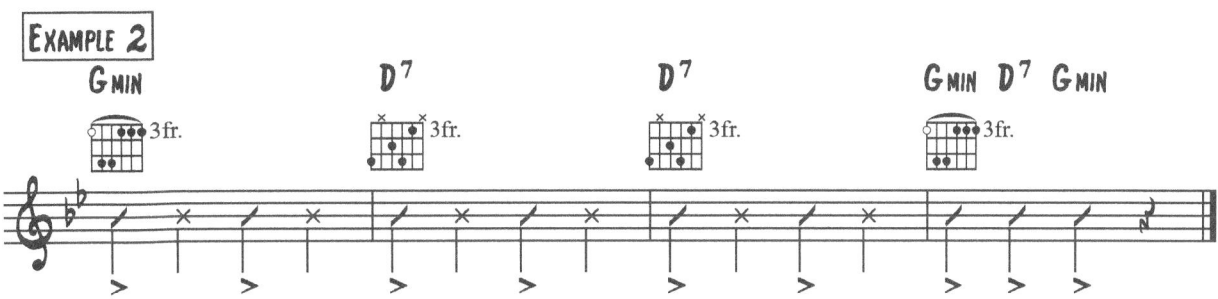

TRY INTEGRATING THE TWO FIRST SAMPLES INTO A COMMON PROGRESSION AND MELODY NOW.

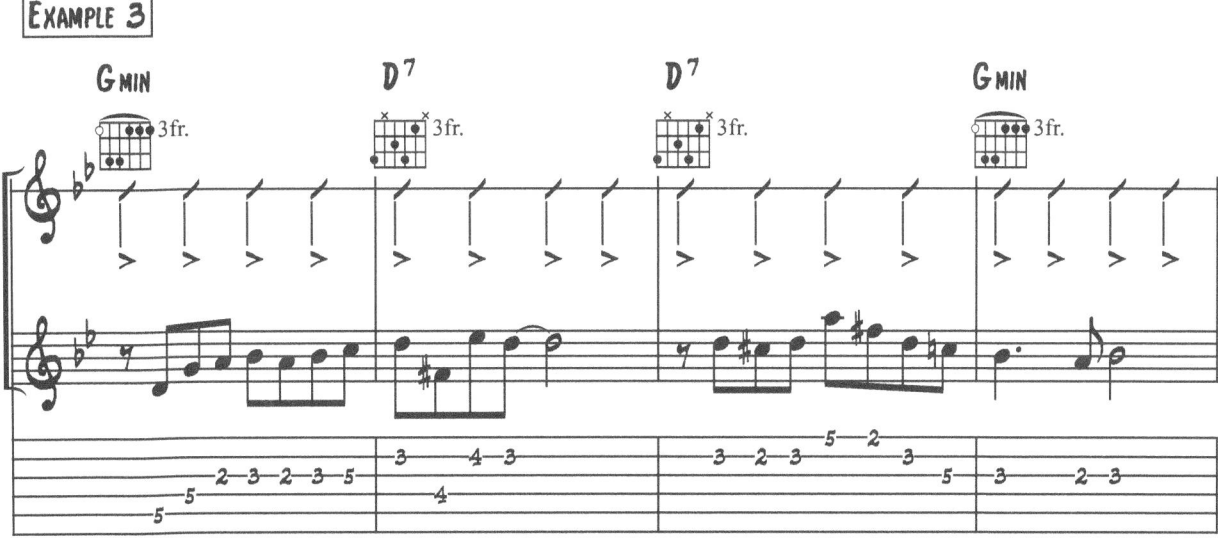

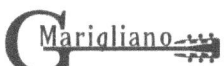

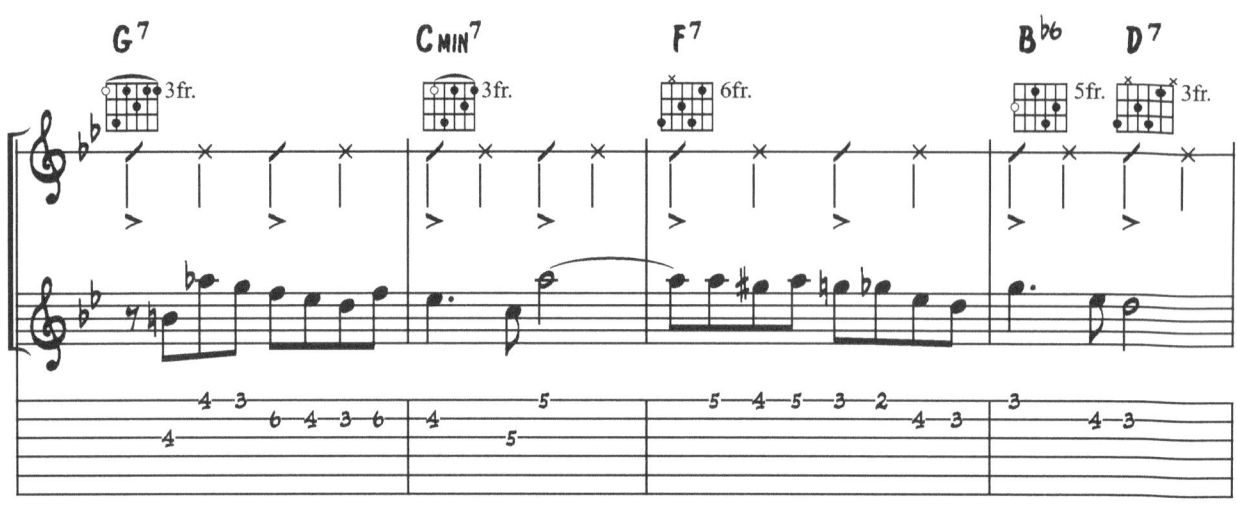

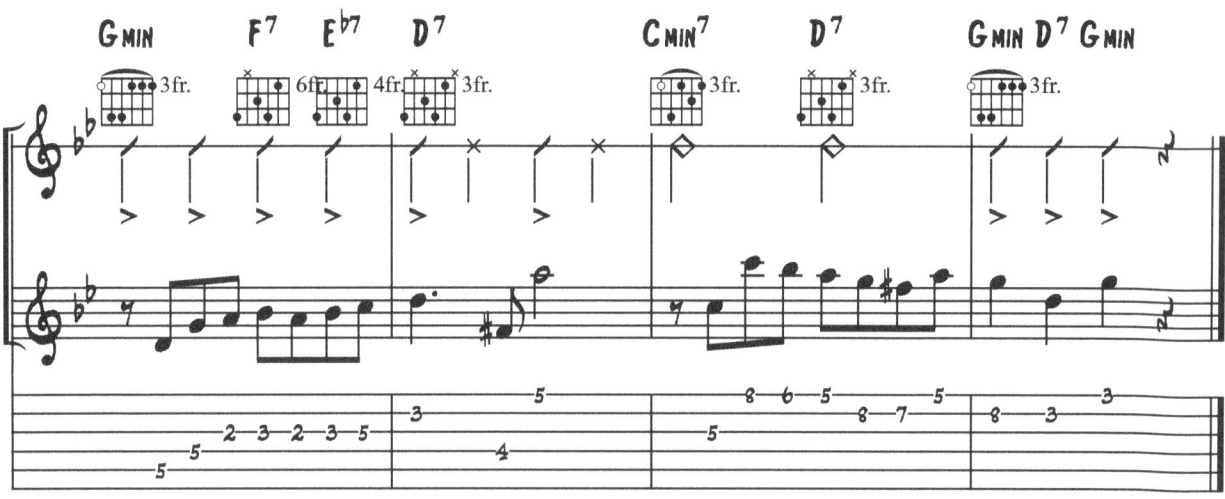

"MARCATO IN TWO TIMES WITH BASS LINE FEEL," SIMILAR TO THE MARCATO IN TWO TIMES, WE STRIKE THE FOUR QUARTER NOTE BEATS, PLAYING THE CHORD ONLY ON BEATS 1 AND 3, BUT INSTEAD OF MUTING BEATS 2 AND 4, WE HIT ONLY THE LOWER STRINGS, ATTEMPTING TO SOUND LIKE A BASS.

EXAMPLE 4

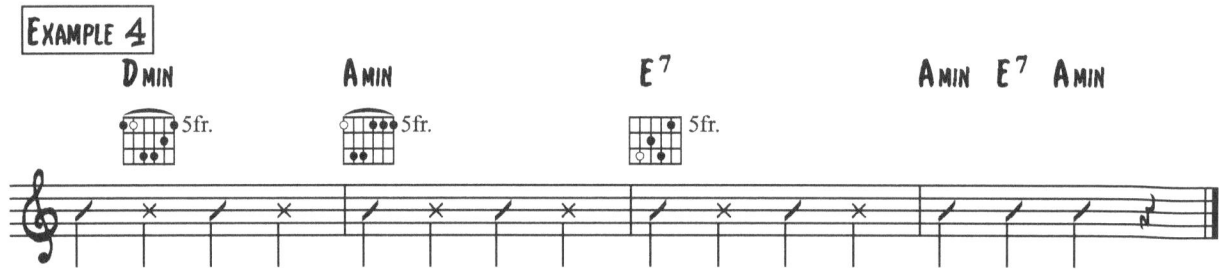

NOW LET'S ADD THE GLISS UP TO THE CHORD; THIS IS A REALLY CRUCIAL ITEM TO LEARN AND USE BECAUSE IT'S PART OF THE TANGO COMPING SENSATION. ON BEAT 4, WE WILL MAKE A GLISS ALONG THE FRETBOARD, BLOCKING/MUTING THE STRINGS AND PLAYING THE CHORD THAT WE WILL PLAY ON BEAT 1 OF THE FOLLOWING BAR.

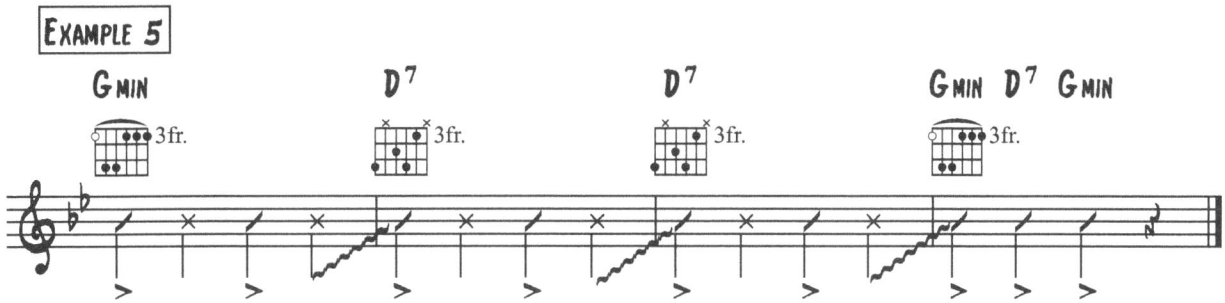

* PRACTICE THIS PATTERN WITH OTHER CHORD PROGRESSIONS

HALF NOTE COMPING: THIS COMPING TECHNIQUE IS MOSTLY USED WHEN WE HAVE TWO CHORDS PER MEASURE, ON SLOW PASSAGES IN THE MIDDLE OF A SONG, INTROS, AND IT ALSO HELPS US INCORPORATE A BASS LINE BY CREATING CHORD SUBSTITUTIONS.

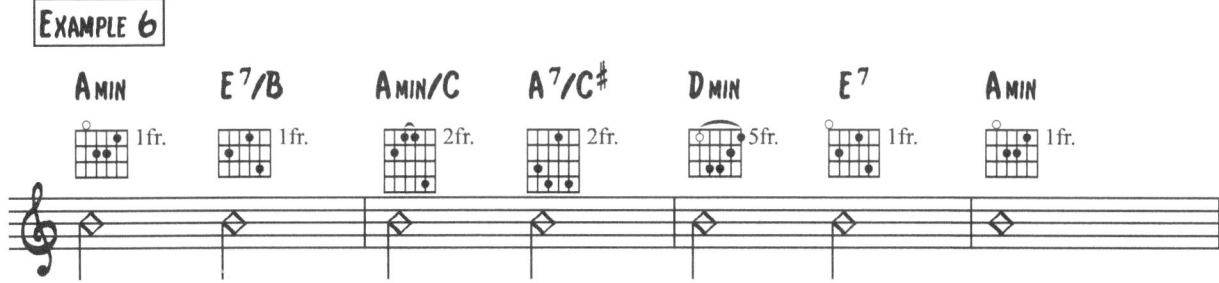

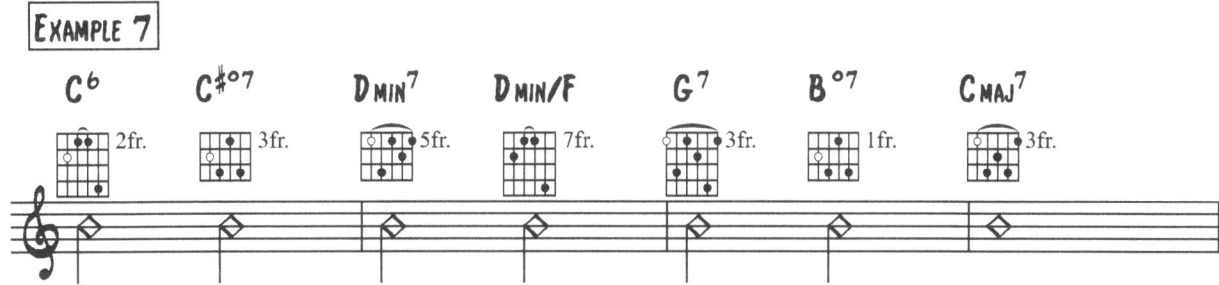

SYNCOPATION: AFTER LEARNING THE GLISS, WE CAN ADD WHAT IS KNOWN AS SYNCOPATION IN TANGO AND PLAY IT TOGETHER; THIS IS THE MOST CLASSIC SOUND ON TANGO COMPING, ESPECIALLY ON THE STRONG PARTS OF A SONG. THIS IS THE BASSIC SYNCOPATION ON RHYTHM, AND NOTICE HOW I HIT THE LOWER STRINGS OVER THE EIGHT NOTES AND THE HIGH STRINGS ON THE QUARTER NOTES:

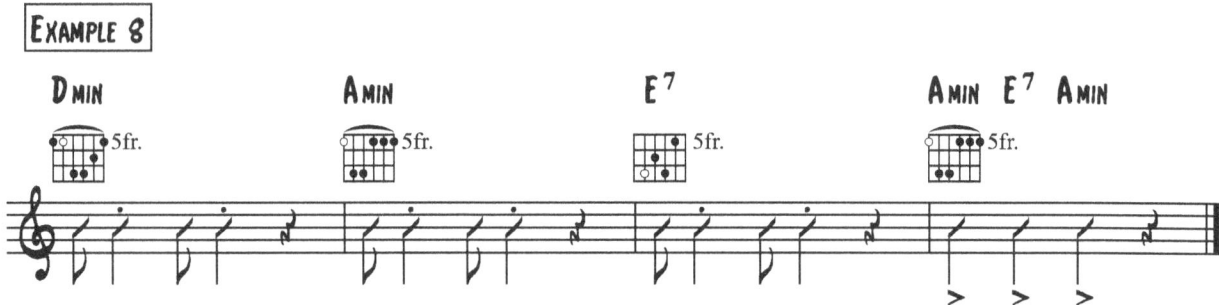

NOW, IN 99% OF SONGS, THIS SYNCOPATION IS PLAYED AS A GLISS UP BLOCKING/MUTING STRINGS, AT THE LAST EIGHT NOTE OFF TH FOUR BEAT AT THE PREVIOUS MEASURE. I'M GOING TO INCLUDE SOMETHING WE'LL LOOK AT IN THE NEXT CHAPTER: A LINE AT THE END AS A LINK PASSAGE TO ANOTHER SECTION OR AS THE END OF A SONG.

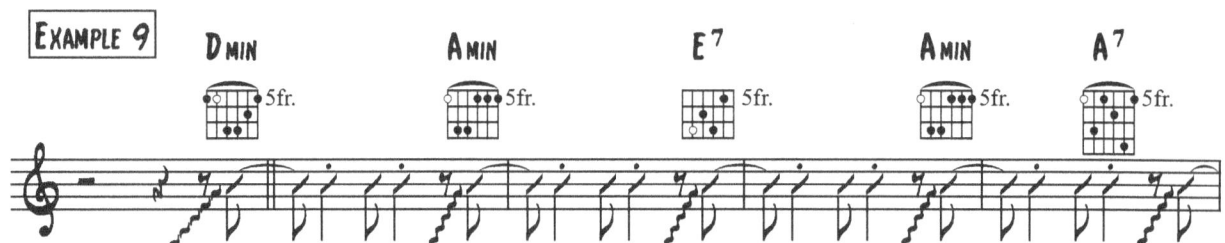

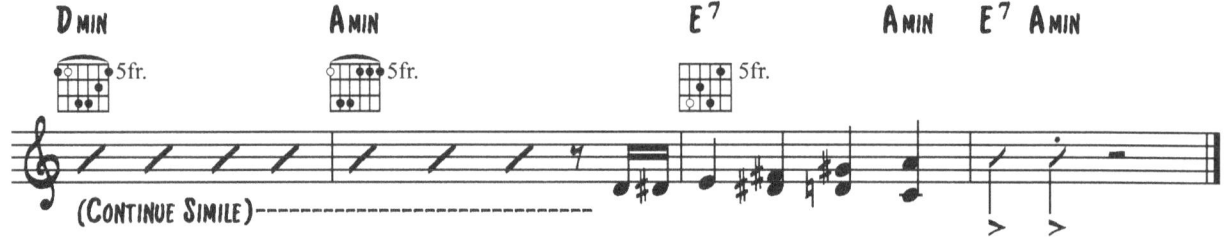

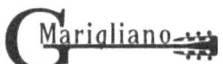

CHAPTER 2
LINKING UP MUSICAL PASSAGES

On this chapter we are going to study those link phrases that are very common on Tango style, and will give to us this characteristic sound that we found mostly at the end of a song, or at the middle of a song section.

This kind of prhases too, are going to be very helpfull to change the tempo, making a pause and change the rhythm feel for the next section, in Tango music it's very common to have a verse in a major key and the chorus section doing a modulation to minor key on the same root

We can use the next line to end on a major or a minor chord, we only need to change the 3rd on last chord

Another variation is to play the descending melody an octave higher, and below them the ascending scale notes, also works for major and minor resolution changing the last note.

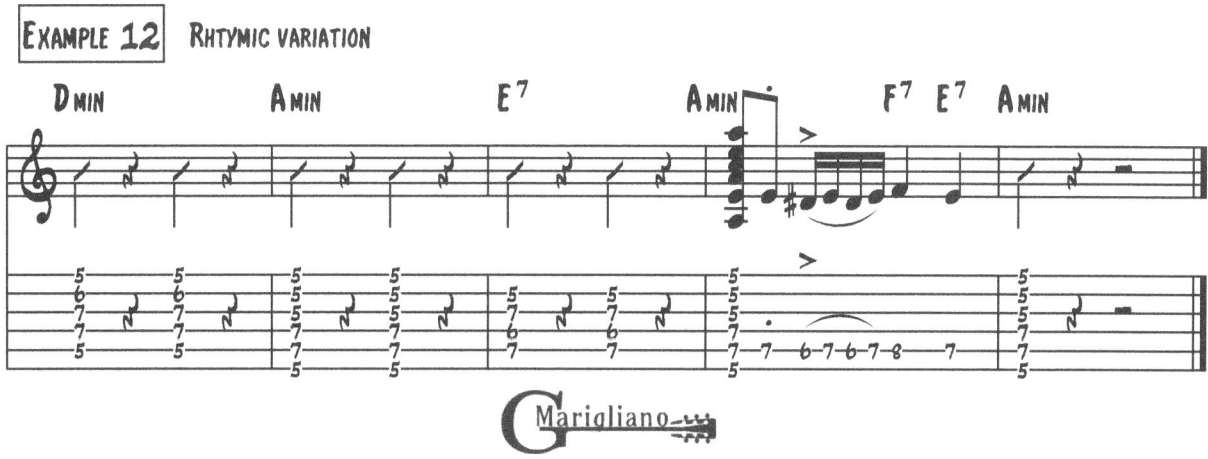

Marigliano

EXAMPLE 13 RHYMTIC VARIATION ON A DIFFERENT POSITION AT THE END AND PLAYING THE CHORDS

EXAMPLE 14 ANOTHER RHYTMIC VARIATION STARTING ON THE 5TH NOTE OF THE ROOT CHORD

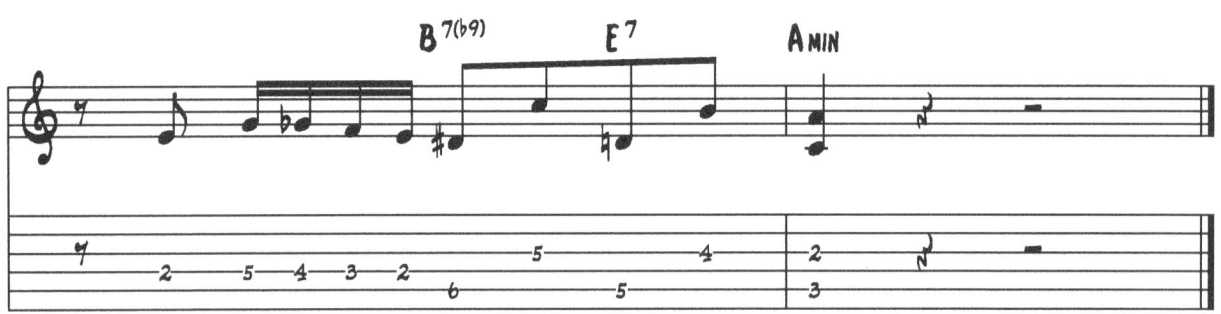

EXAMPLE 15 AN OCTAVE HIGHER

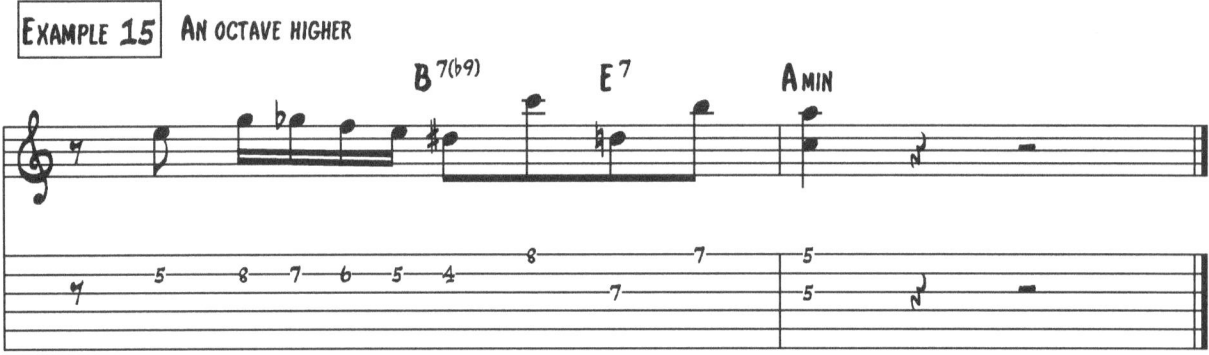

EXAMPLE 16 ADDING THE CHORDS AT THE END

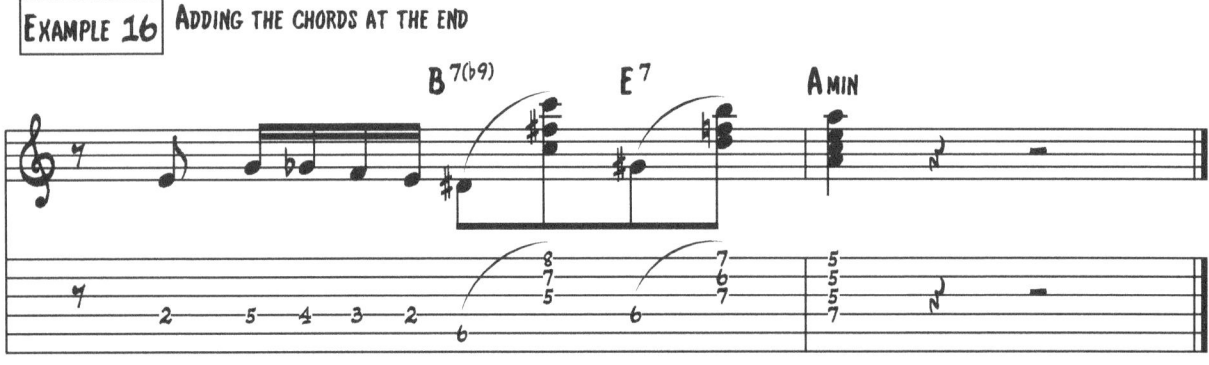

EXAMPLE 17 "OCTAVES"

EXAMPLE 18

EXAMPLE 19 | NEXT IT'S AN EXAMPLE OVER A COMMON PROGRESSION IN THE KEY OF D MINOR USING LINKING PHRASES ON THE UPPER STRINGS AND THE EXAMPLE 10 TRANSPOSED TO THIS KEY.

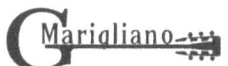

CONECTING THE I TO V USING CHORDS IN MINOR AND MAJOR KEY, AND LINKING PHRASES

EXAMPLE 20

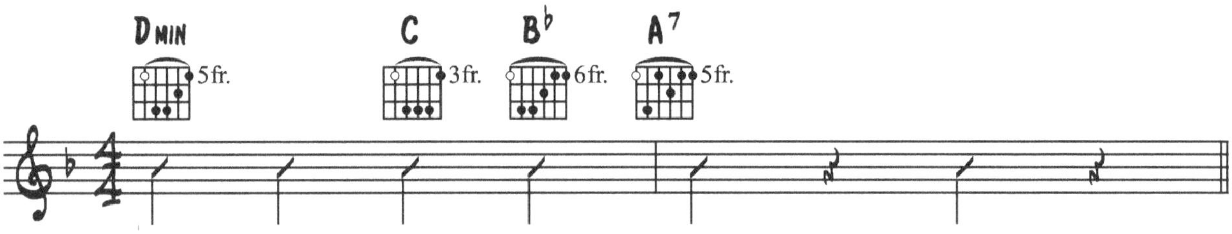

EXAMPLE 21

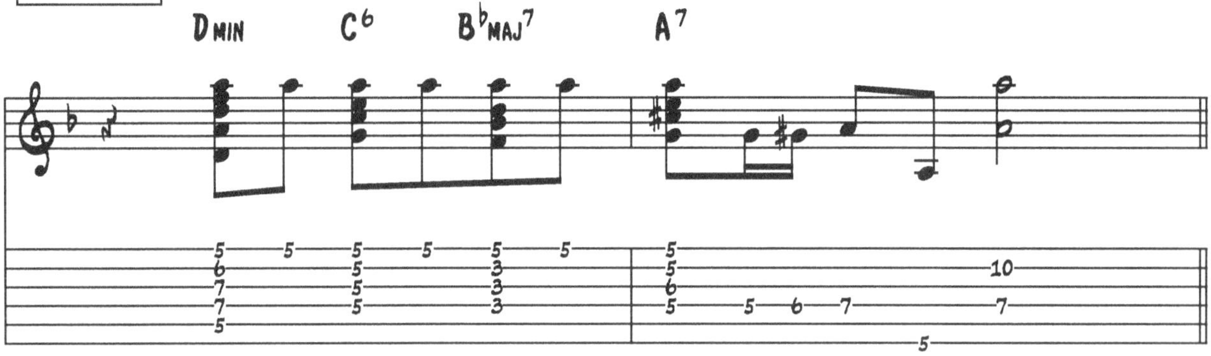

EXAMPLE 22

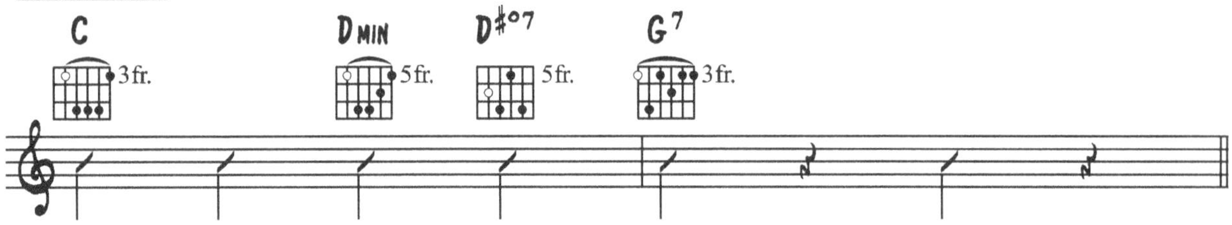

EXAMPLE 23

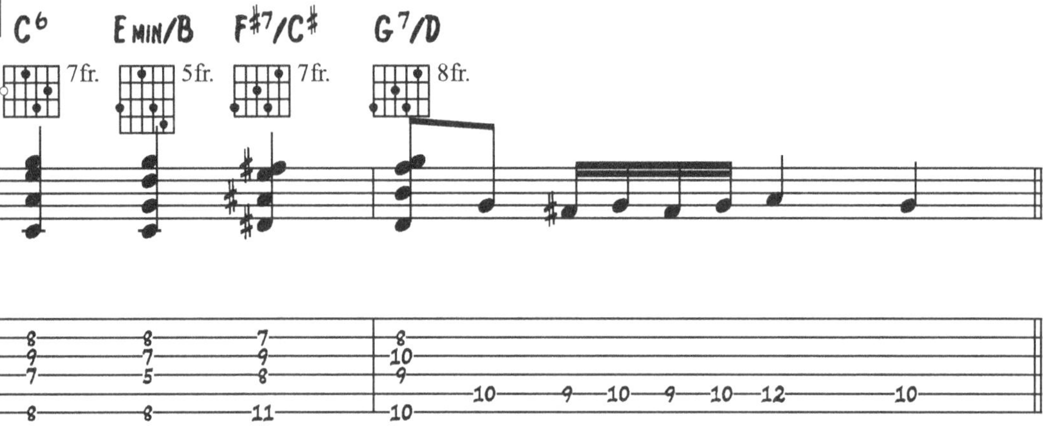

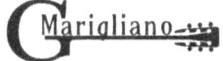

CHAPTER 3
SUBSTITUTIONS

THIS IS AN IMPORTANT ABILITY TO LEARN ON THE GUITAR. WE WILL HAVE A STRONG RESOURCE TO BUILD OUR TANGO COMPING IF WE CAN HANDLE THIS.

I MUST EMPHASIZE THAT THIS METHOD OF GUITAR COMPING IS NOT EXCLUSIVE TO TANGO MUSIC; SIMILAR PATTERNS MAY BE FOUND IN JAZZ, POP, AND OTHER FOLK MUSICS. THE ONLY ASPECT OF THIS THAT WILL CHANGE IS THE BEAT AND THE WAY IN WHICH WE ARRANGE THE SUBSTITUTES TO SOUND LIKE TANGO ACCOMPANIMENT.

SO, WE HAVE THREE IMPORTANT CHORD FAMILIES THAT WE WILL DISCOVER ON EVERY TUNE:

MAJOR, MINOR, AND DOMINANT 7 CHORDS, AND THOSE ARE THE CHORDS THAT WE WILL BE LEARNING.

EXAMPLE 24 | MAJOR CHORDS SUBTITUTIONS, ROOTS ON 6TH AND 5TH STRINGS

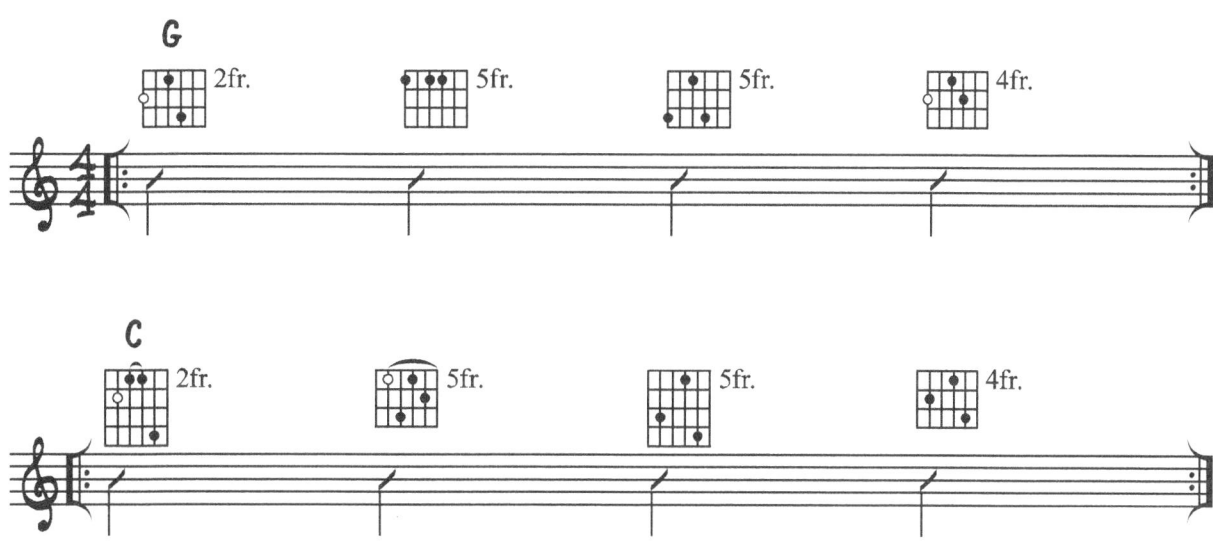

EXAMPLE 25 | MINOR CHORDS SUBTITUTIONS, ROOTS ON 6TH AND 5TH STRINGS

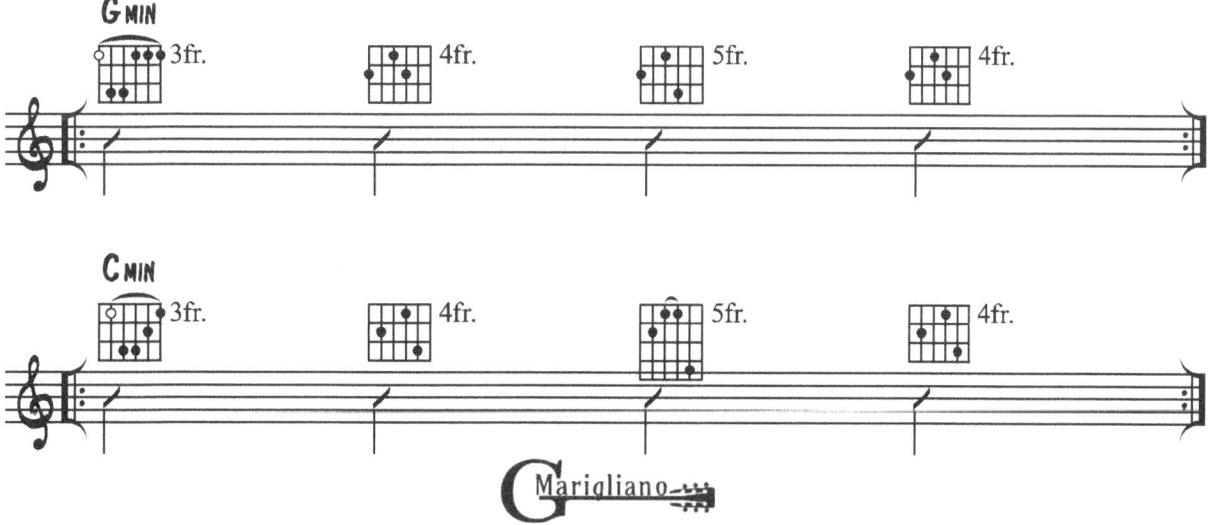

EXAMPLE 26 DOMINANT 7 CHORDS SUBTITUTIONS, ROOTS ON 6TH AND 5TH STRINGS

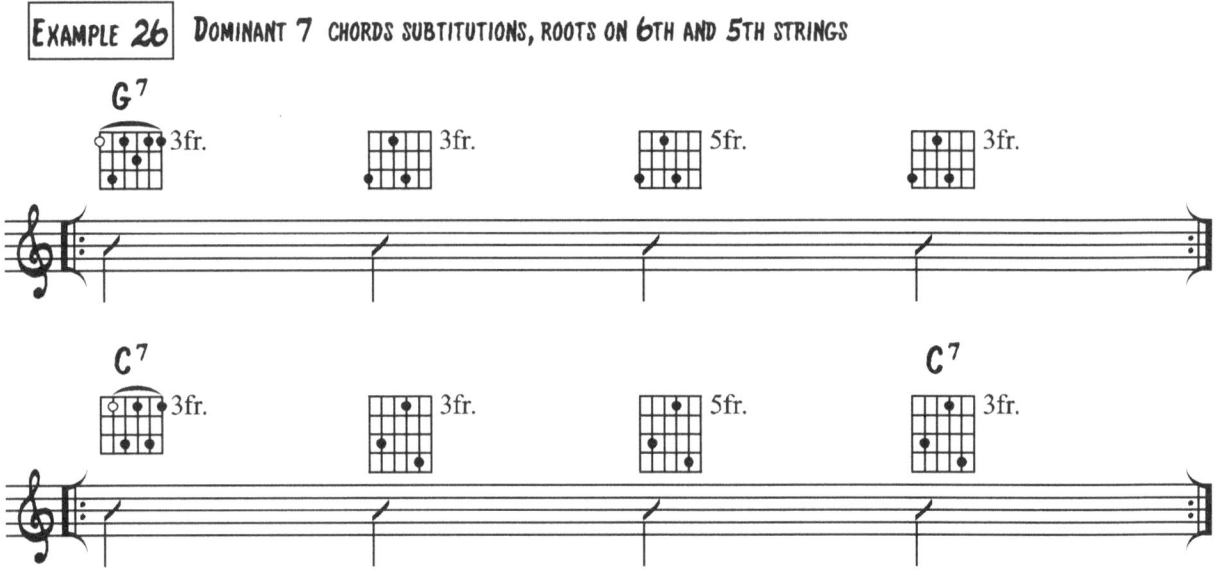

IN THE TWO FOLLOWING EXAMPLES, WE WILL BE USING SUBSTITUTIONS OVER TWO MOST COMMON MAJOR AND MINOR PROGRESSIONS.
WE SHOULD LEARN THAT, AS SHOWN IN THE EXAMPLES, WE DON'T ALWAYS NEED TO USE ENTIRE CHORDS FOR SUBSTITUTIONS.
IT WILL ALSO DEPEND ON THE RHYTHM WE USE.

EXAMPLE 27

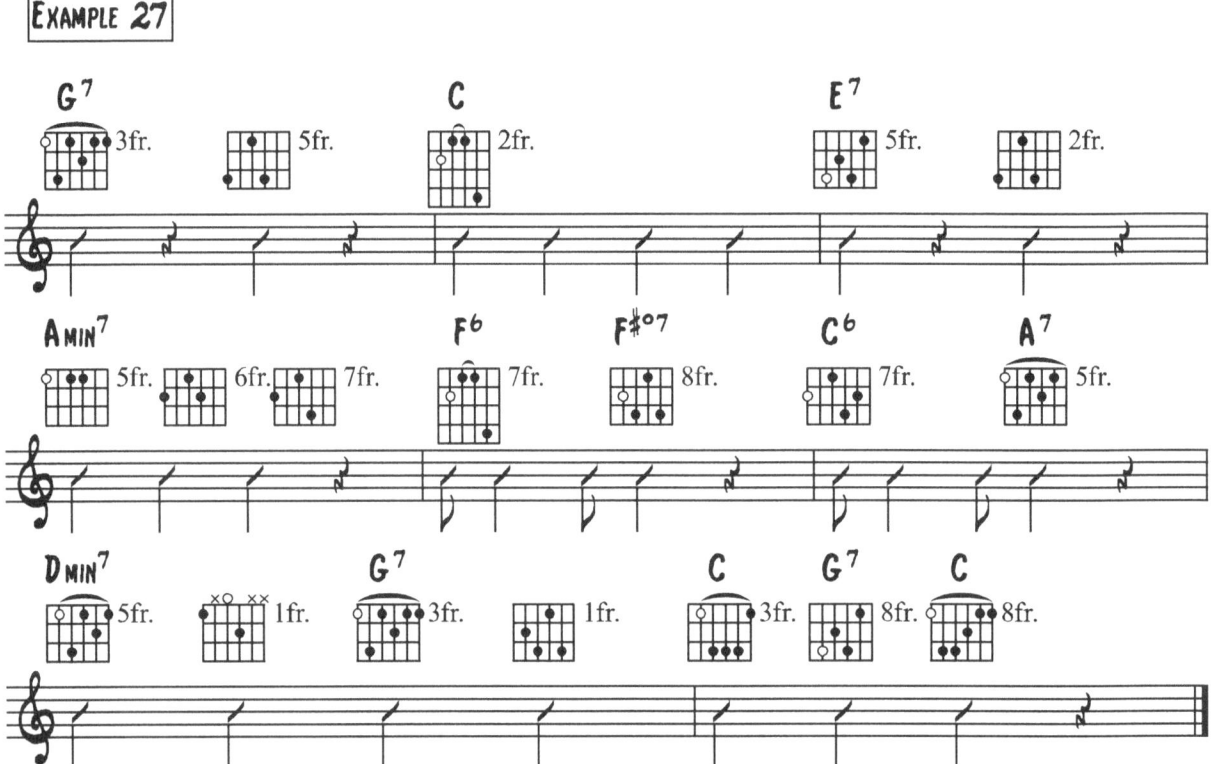

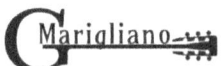

EXAMPLE 28

DMIN
5fr.
C
3fr.
B♭
6fr.
A7
5fr.
5fr.
7fr.
7fr.
1. DMIN
5fr.
6fr.
7fr.
B♭7
6fr.
2. DMIN
5fr.
D7
3fr.
GMIN
3fr.
4fr.
5fr.
A7
5fr.
DMIN
5fr.
C
3fr.
B♭
6fr.
A7
5fr.
A7
10fr.
DMIN7
10fr.

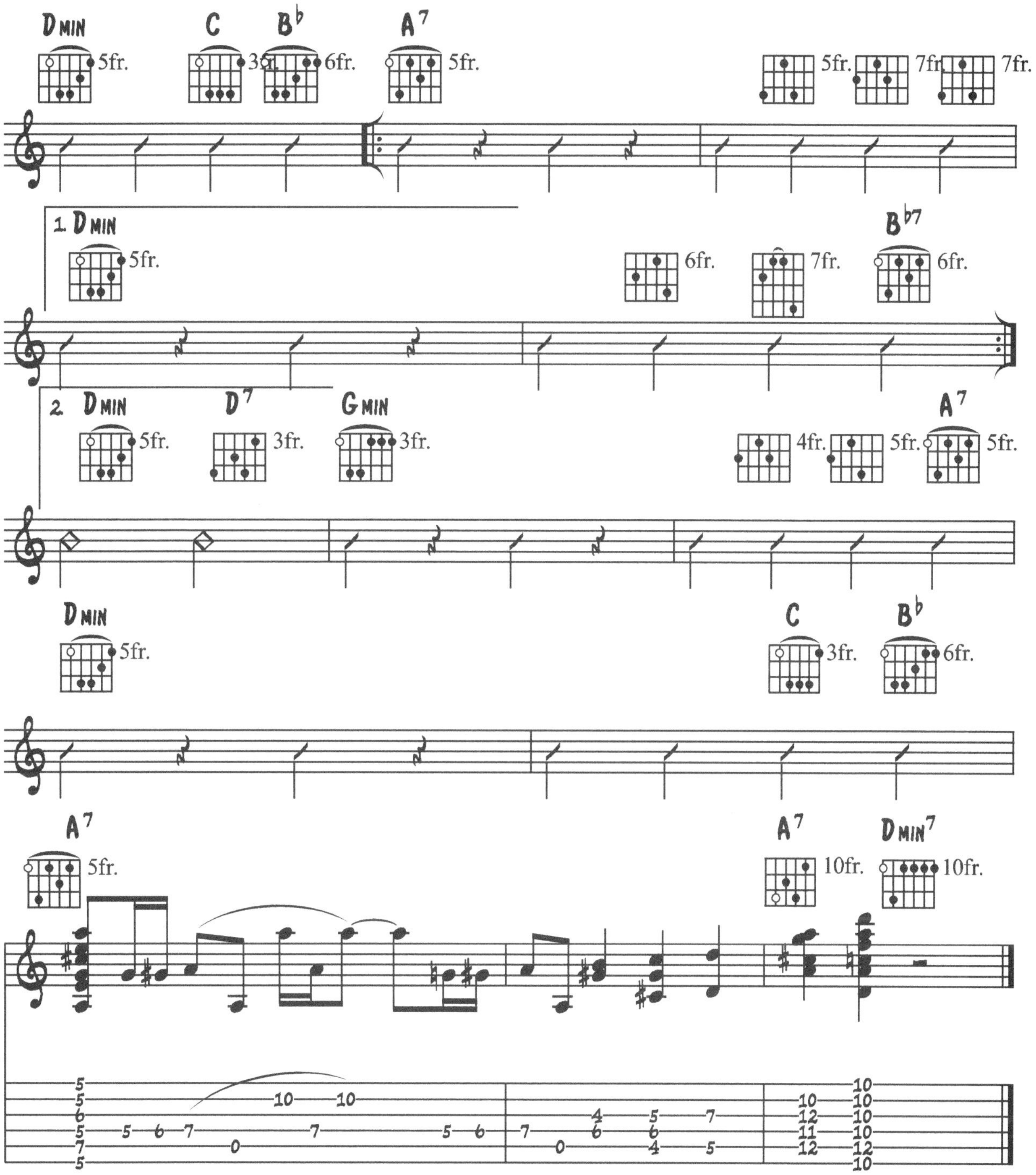

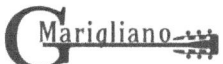

CHAPTER 4
WALKING

FOLLOWING THE STUDY OF SUBSTITUTIONS, ANOTHER TECHNIQUE THAT WE MUST INCORPORATE IS THE WALKING BASS.
WHILE THE WALKING BASS IN JAZZ USES MORE CHROMATICH NOTES TO APPROACH THE ROOT OF THE NEXT CHORD, IN TANGO
WE ARE GOING TO USE SUBTITUTIONS AND SOMETHING NAMED "ADORNOS" ON THE BASS LINE TO LINK OUR CHORD PROGRESSION.

WALKING BASS IS TYPICALLY USED WHEN WE HAVE TWO CHORDS ON EACH BAR

THE BASS LINE WILL BE PLAYED WITH THE THUMB OF OUR RIGHT HAND, AND THE REST OF OUR FINGERS WILL CREATE A RHYTHM
COUNTERPOINT BY PLAYING THE REST OF THE CHORD NOTES.

AT THIS POINT, WE USE THE RHYTHM VARIATIONS WE LEARNED TOO IN PREVIOUS CHAPTERS WHILE LEARNING AND INCORPORATING
THE NEW ONES.

EXAMPLE 29

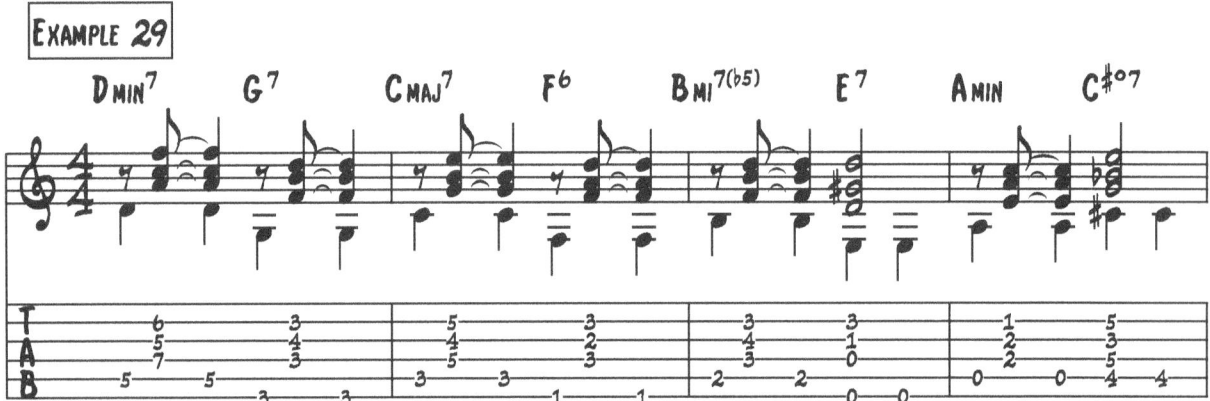

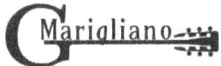

EXAMPLE 30

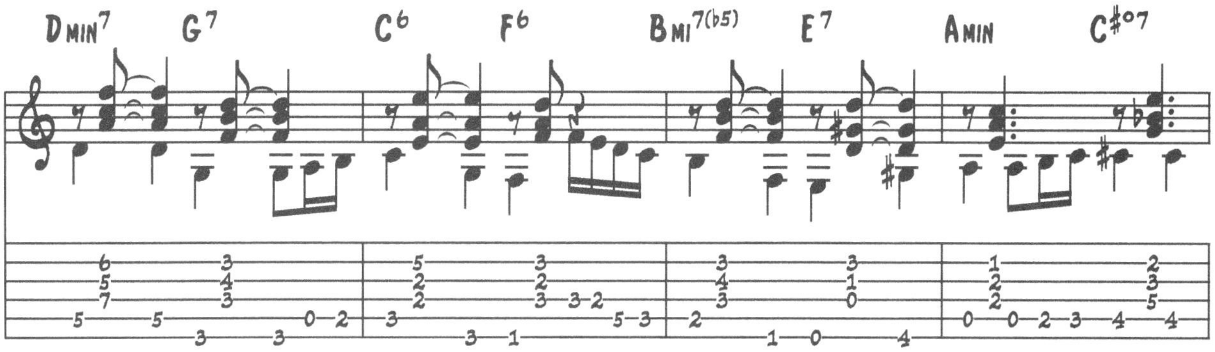

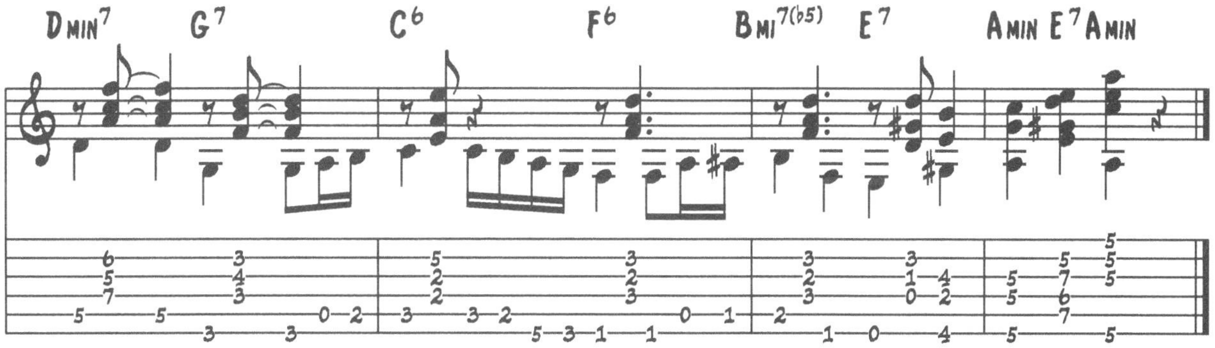

EXAMPLE 31

Amin7
A7
Dmin7
%
Gliss.
Amin7
Bmi7(b5)
E7
Amin7
E7
Amin
Gliss.

Example 32

A6
E7
A6
A6
A7
D
Bmin7
E7
A
E7
A
A6

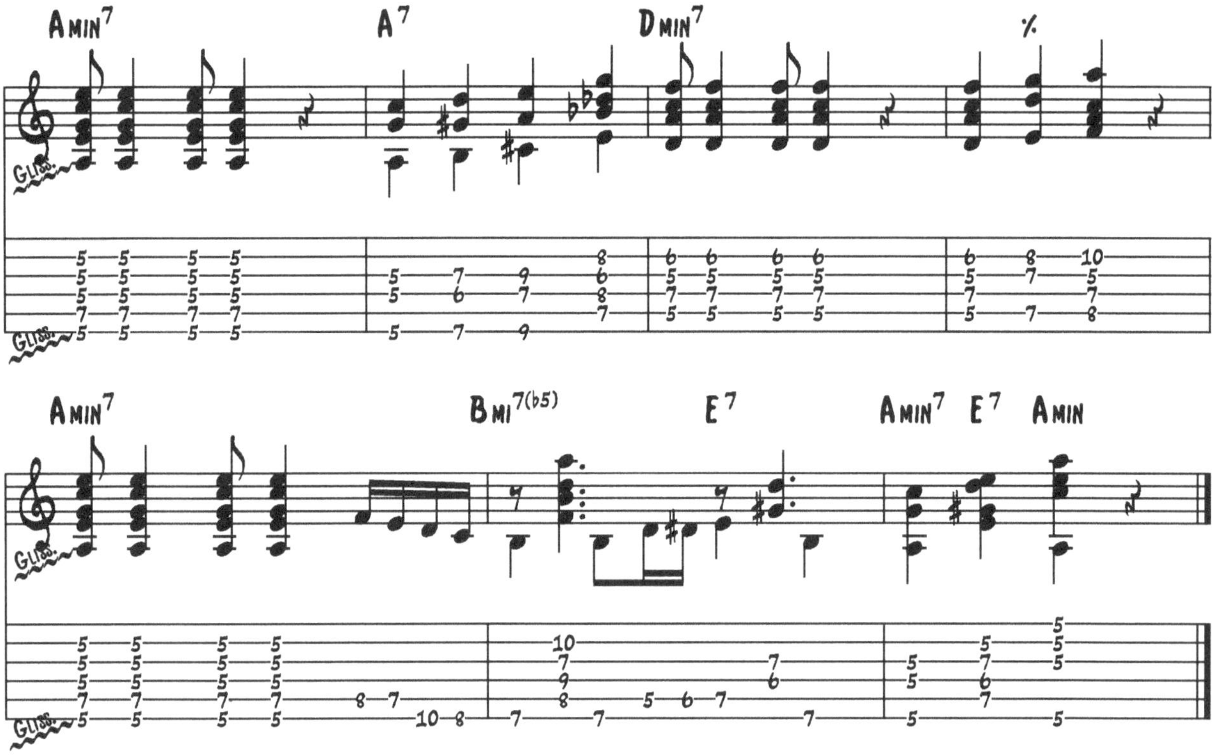

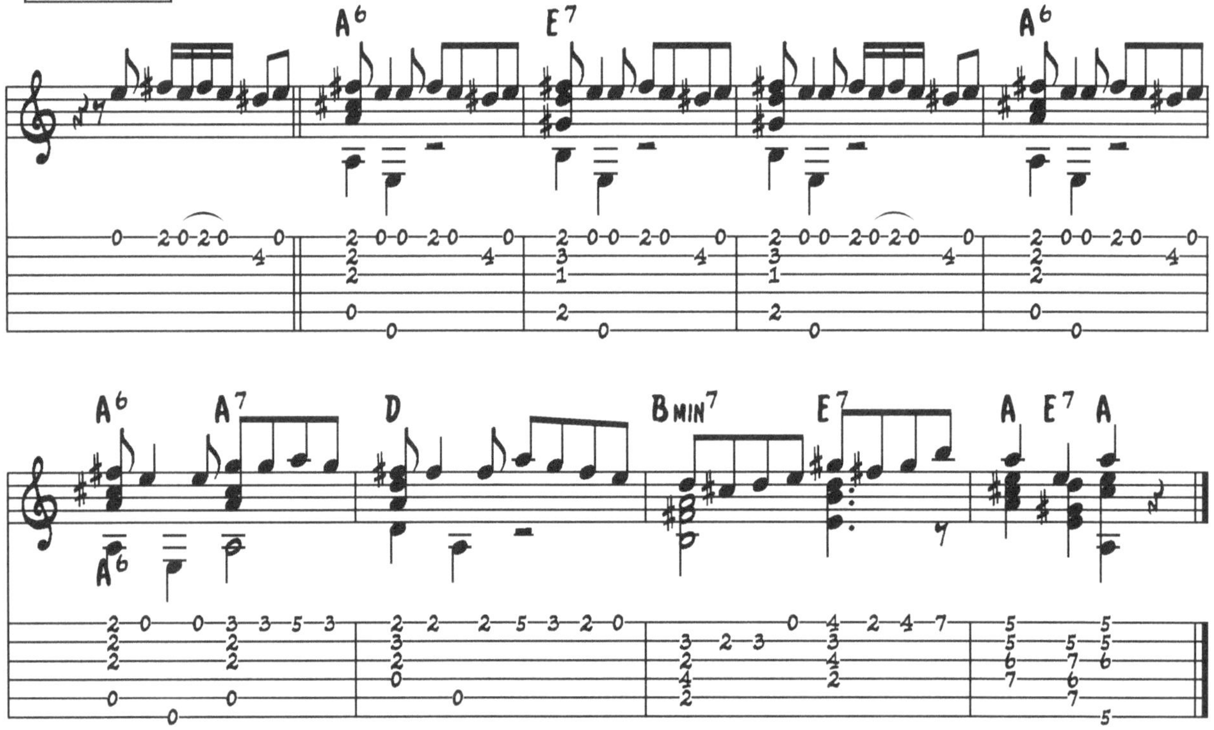

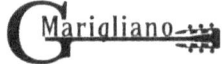

CHAPTER 5

INSIDE TANGO

As we progress in this style, we will discover that, like all styles, it requires us to work hard if we want to achieve good tango comping; we must learn different progressions, chord substitutions, and complete songs that will be beyond the scope of this book.

In this final chapter, we'll look at some more Tango progressions, putting everything we've learned so far together. We'll go over chord melody phrases that we can use as introductions, finals, melodic lines that we can use to connect different chords as well as some traditional tango song sections.

EXAMPLE 33

Tango accompaniment in the style of a bandoneon, based on Anibal Troilo's composition "Te Llaman Malevo."

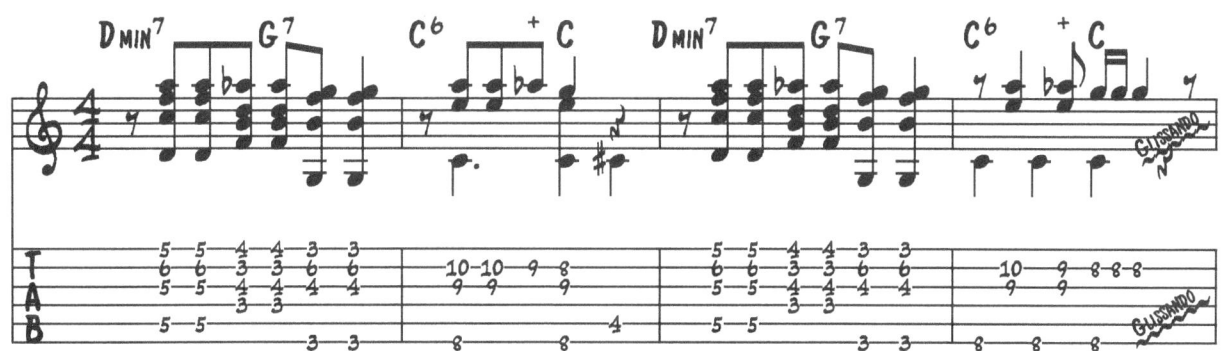

Example 34

A walking bass technique that can be used over the verse chord progressions of the tango "Mariposita."

Example 35 "Pesante" "Syncopa" and "Marcato" technique for Tango progression "Malena"

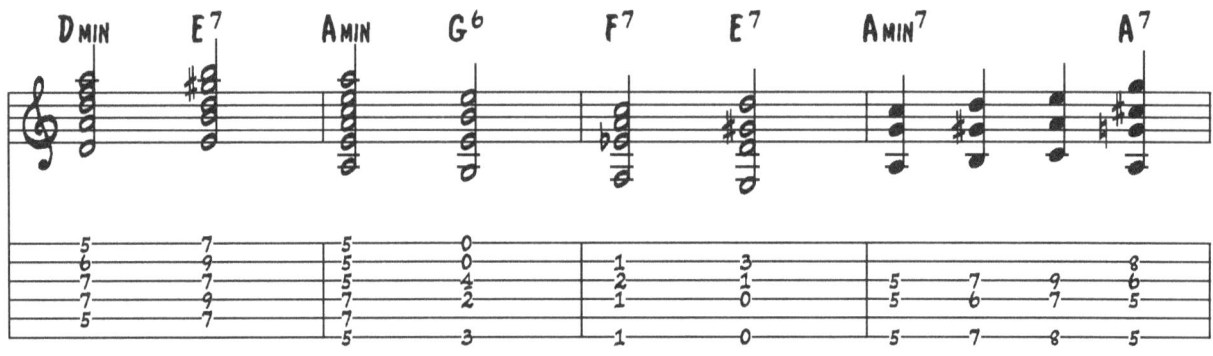

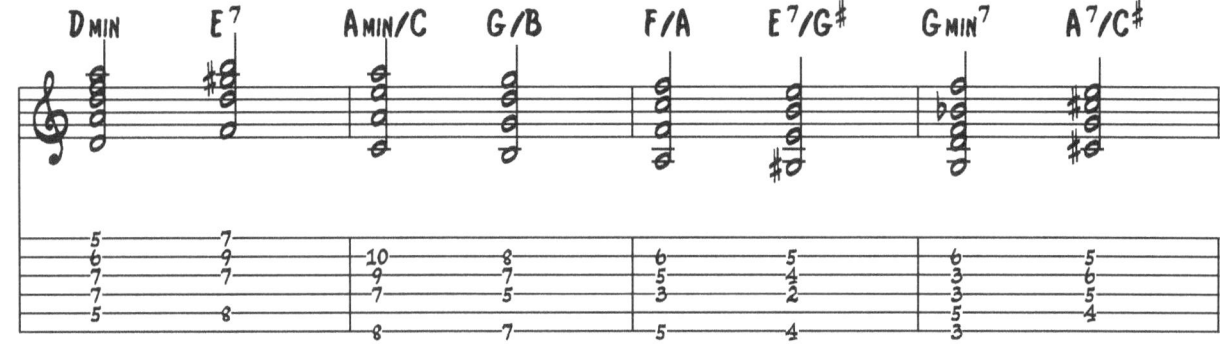

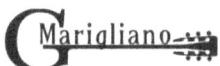

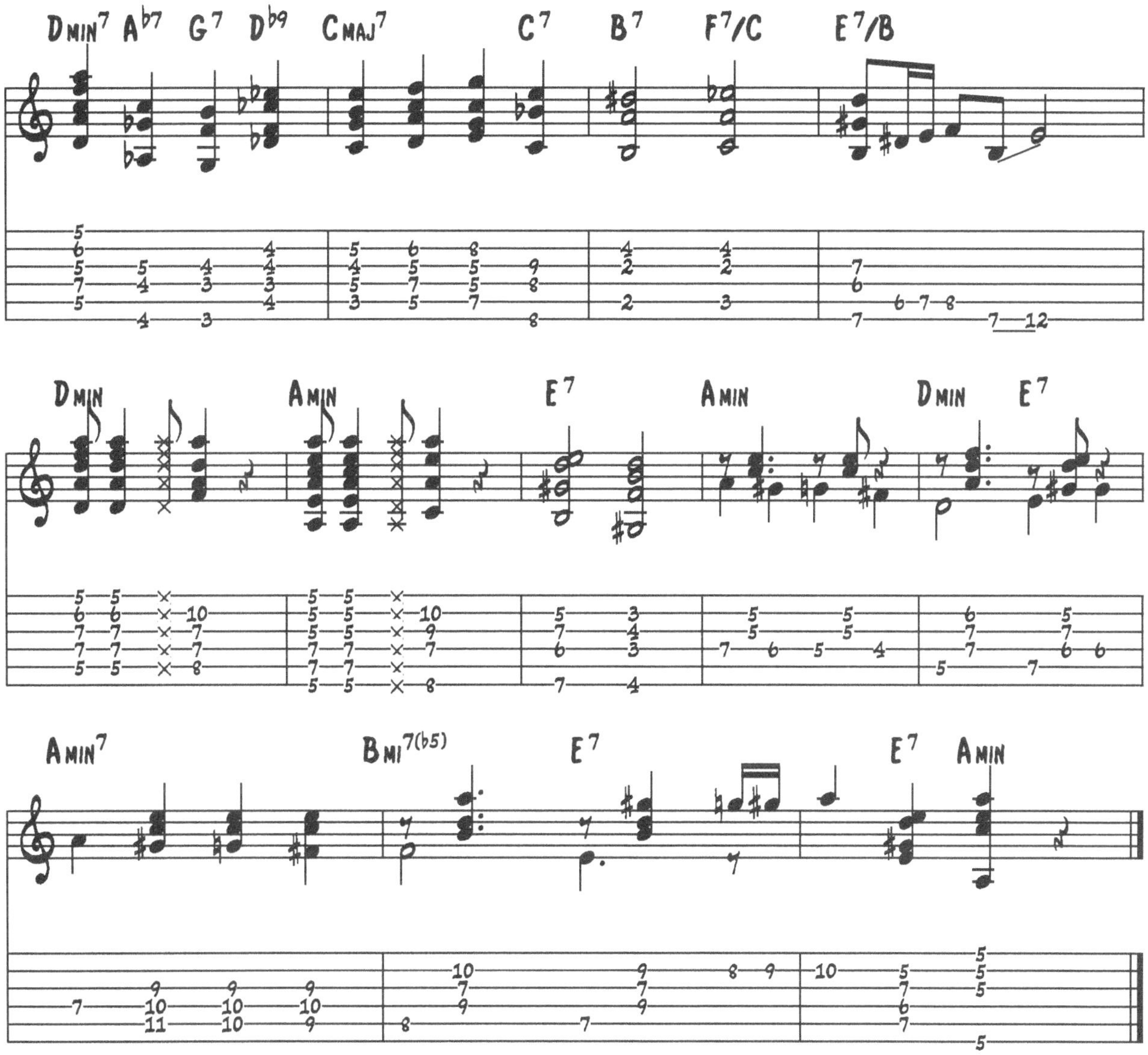

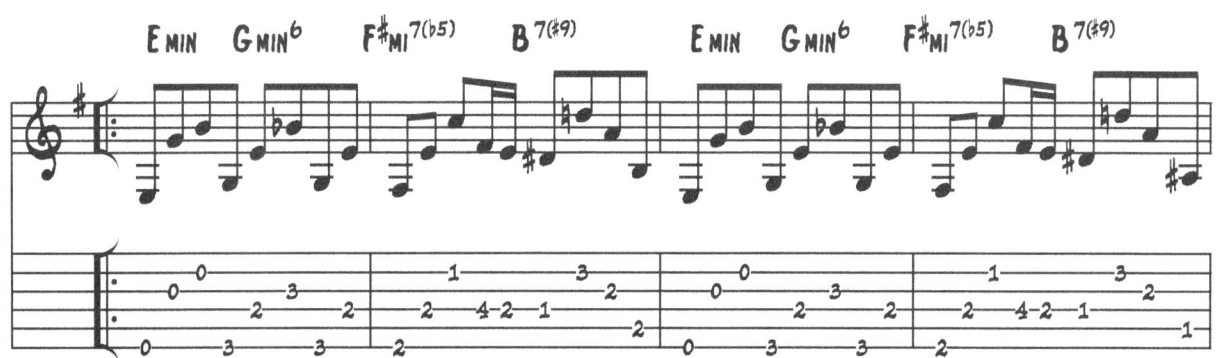

Example 36　3+3+2 Clave, Astor Piazzolla Style

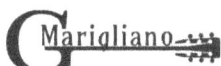

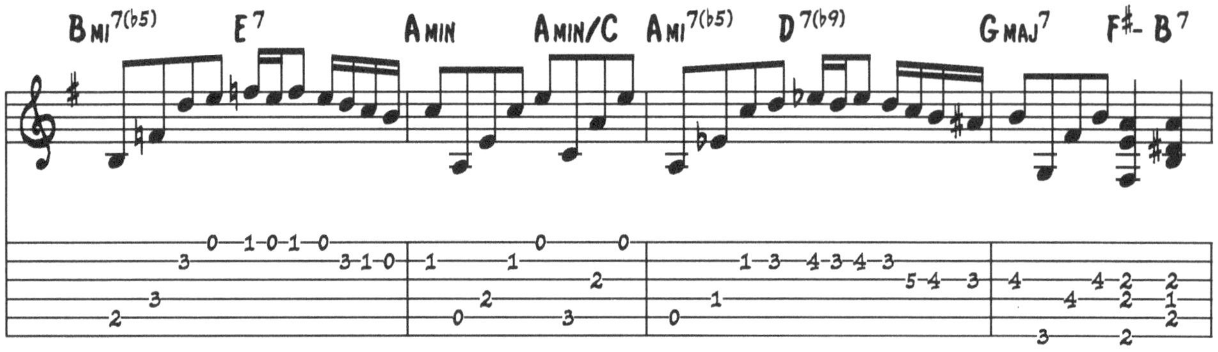

Bmi⁷⁽ᵇ⁵⁾   E⁷   Amin   Amin/C   Ami⁷⁽ᵇ⁵⁾   D⁷⁽ᵇ⁹⁾   Gmaj⁷   F♯- B⁷

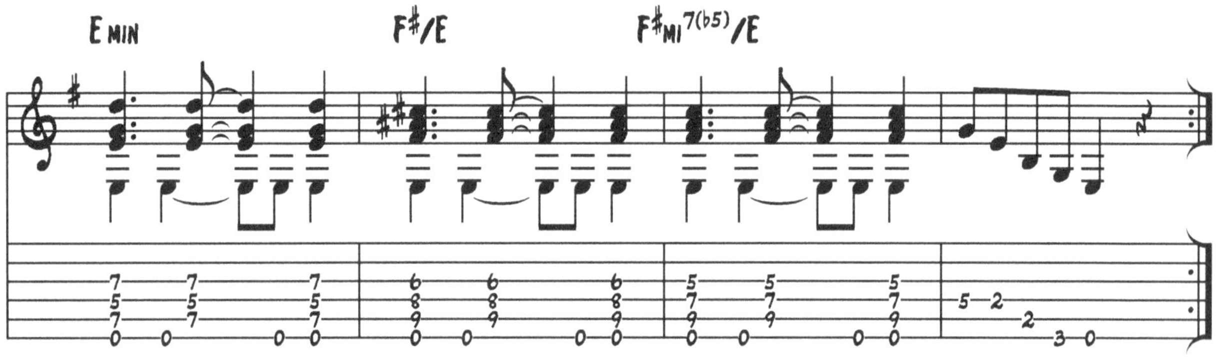

Emin   F♯/E   F♯mi⁷⁽ᵇ⁵⁾/E

EXAMPLE 37 PIAZZOLLA STYLE

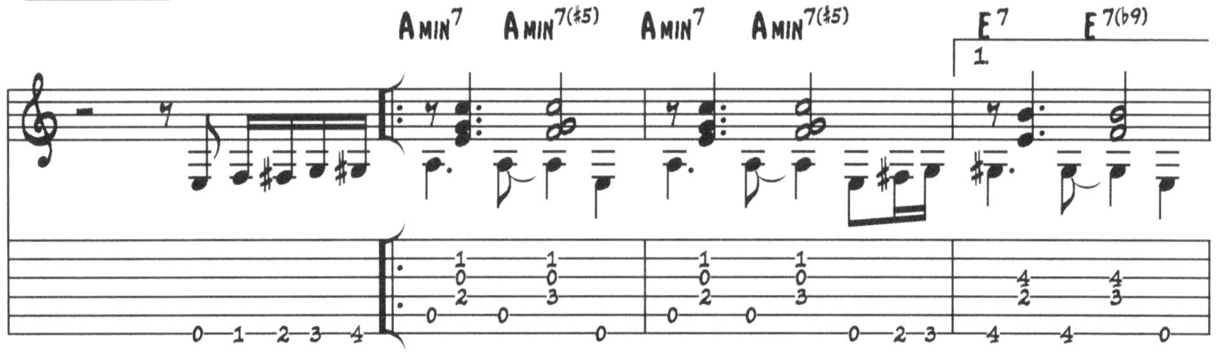

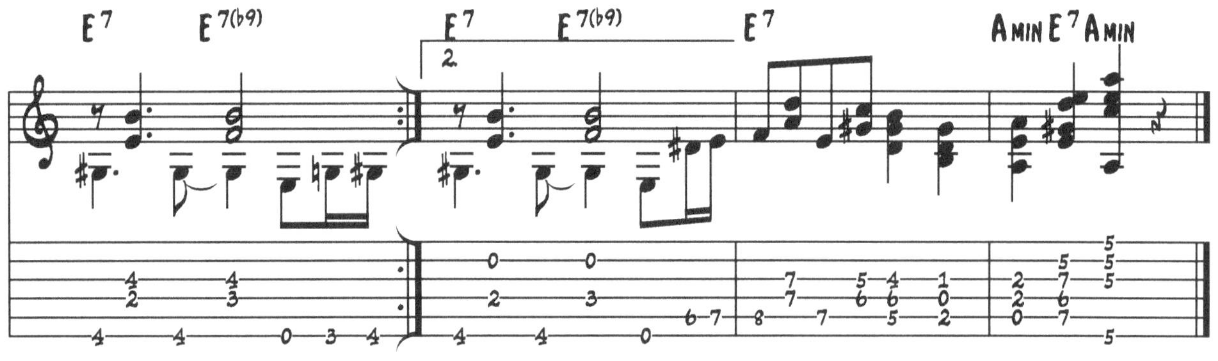

Amin⁷   Amin⁷⁽♯⁵⁾   Amin⁷   Amin⁷⁽♯⁵⁾   E⁷   E⁷⁽ᵇ⁹⁾

E⁷   E⁷⁽ᵇ⁹⁾   E⁷   E⁷⁽ᵇ⁹⁾   E⁷   Amin E⁷ Amin

LISTENING TO AND LEARNING FROM THE CARLOS GARDEL RECORDINGS IS EXTREMELY BENEFICIAL. THE GUITARS ON GARDEL'S RECORDING ARE PURE TANGO, AND YOU WILL BE ABLE TO FOLLOW THE ORIGINAL 1933 RECORDING ARRANGEMENT ON THE FOLLOWING TRANSCRIPTION OF THE SONG "MELODIA DE ARRABAL."

EXAMPLE 38

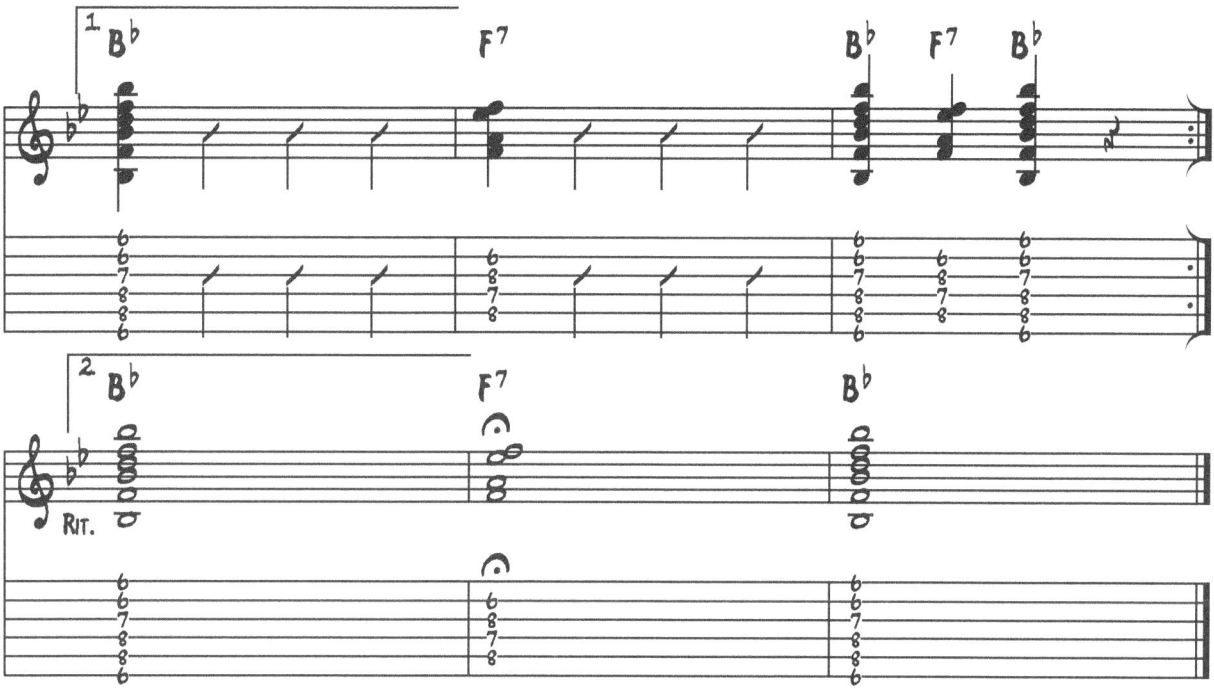

FINALE:

A DISTINCTIVE FEATURE OF TANGO IS THE CLASSIC SOUND AT THE END OF THE SONG, WHICH IS USUALLY PLAYED BY ALL INSTRUMENTS. WHETHER THE COMPOSITION ENDS IN A MAJOR OR MINOR CHORD, THE LINE PRECEDING THE FINAL CHORD BEGINS AT THE ROOT OF THE FIFTH GRADE AND IS A CHROMATICH LINE TO THE TONALITY'S ROOT. LET'S GOING TO LEARN THE CLASSICS AND SOME VARIATIONS.

EXAMPLE 39

www.ingramcontent.com/pod-product-compliance
Lightning Source LLC
Chambersburg PA
CBHW041647120626
46551CB00016B/2336